Reality
Check

Danielle Pitter

For my younger self,
who never stopped dreaming.

Copyright © 2021 Danielle Pitter

ISBN: 9798483168461

Excerpt from The Twilight Saga: Eclipse (2010), by Melissa Rosenberg

Design: Margherita Buzzi
Typeset in Adobe Garamond Pro

www.poetrybooksya.com

Table of contents

Part I
Emotion

Part II
Time

Part III
Self

Preface

When I was a child, I could never call myself a writer. I'd always thought I had to be known by everyone, loved by millions, with a number one spot on The New York Times bestseller list. I'd always found other jobs, only to come back to the one thing I'd always run away from, writing. Sure, I'd dabbled in writing poetry and short stories before, even fanfiction, but there was always this part of me that wished for more. Wanted more. To be more, meant that I had to stop letting the fear, anxiety, and failures get in the way of what I wanted.

With the global pandemic still on the rise, it was the perfect time for me to wake myself up and finally take a chance to try something that has been on my mind since forever, my first published piece of work.

These poems started on Patreon, but I thought they'd look and feel better here in one space, altogether for everyone to read. I hope you enjoy reading them as much as I enjoyed writing them.

Part I
Emotion

Emotional Closet

Yesterday, I did something that had been on the back of my mind for ages.
Cleaned out my closet.
Not only did I clean out my physical closet,
Full of old dresses, shirts, blouses and pants
That no longer served me.
But also my closet of thoughts and feelings
That no longer served me.
Emotions of the past that didn't funnel my creativity,
How I see myself,
How I see others,
How my truth stands out to me.
It was a grueling, exhausting task.
I thought I wasn't going to keep going, just let
the rest pile
on top of each other.
But I didn't. I knew that if I were to stop, I'd regret
all of this mess I'd made.
I would have had no desire
to complete the job
if I'd stopped when it got hard.
 I kept going until it was done.
Granted, most of the leftover pieces are in bags near me.
Much like the emotions and thoughts of the past.
But at least I can schedule dates to remove the clothes
From my closet. A breath of fresh air soon to come.
A breath of fresh air has come.

Overwhelmed

I'm a bit overwhelmed today,
And all I've been doing is sitting behind a computer
tidying up my bedroom and desk,
and all of this work has done
is make my head hurt.
My eyes sting,
My ears ring,
My back aches,
My body feels tired.
I know all of this
busy work behind the computer
is for a greater cause,
In order to see the bigger picture.
But I wish the process didn't hurt as much.
It's the process of it all that makes me want to...
Not quit, but take yet another break.
A hiatus from the hiatus.

Fresh Start

Welp, this has been a year.
It's not even over yet, and I'm already
ready for it to be over so I can start fresh
again.
Now it's the most important time
Because I'm finally realizing my self-worth.
What I'm capable of,
What I want next,
Who I'm meant to be,
What energy I want to release.

Why do I still feel like I want

more?

More to do.
More to see.
More to be.
More hope.
More love.
More time.

More joy.

More energy.
More to give.
I guess time will tell
And I sure will tell too.

I'm Not Angry Anymore

You fight like your life depends on it,
Like the world would end if you didn't.
The truth is, you're the only one causing your world to end.
There's no one to blame but yourself.
Everyone else can't be wrong.
I don't know how to talk to you
Because it feels like any moment
You'll snap into rage or tears.
Eggshells don't even begin to describe
How it feels to be around you.
It wasn't an easy choice
For you and the girls to move down south,
But you did so anyway.
There is a part of me that does feel sorry for you,
The part that knows you're still the lonely, destroyed soul
Who had to grow up too fast,
Who had to raise both her own inner child and three girls.
I hope those four girls get to grow
In a way that works for them,
With or without you.

Breathe Again

I can breathe properly for the first time in 4 years.
4 years, and God knows how many days, minutes, months, hours.
Who also knows what kind of world I'll walk into now
that the 45th administration is gone, and Biden's has started.
Let's get to work!
With which work will they begin?
So many issues, problems, in the middle of a pandemic.
Racism, women's rights, social justice, inequality, famine,
Healthcare, police reform, climate change—
Can one man or one administration save us from all of this?
Yes... and no.
I think change will come, but slowly.

emotions

I tend to look at people differently now.
My emotions are more aligned with the person I want to be,
Even though the fear is still there,
I don't get upset at people,
Because it's not worth the energy.
Emotions are the investment of energy.
Emotion is what fuels our energy.
It takes too much out of me to match myself with
Someone else.
All it does is waste my emotions and make me exhausted.
So now I come into the world with my best self,
My best emotions, my best form.
Because it's the only form I choose to have.

Part II
Time

The Next Five Years

"Where do you see yourself in five years?"
It's the world's most popular question.
It's also the most annoying question.
I thought I knew the answer,
That I knew where I was going...
But I don't. At least, not yet.
I'm still learning
Where, how and why I see
Myself. And what my truth
Will look like,
Once I tell it.

The next five years...?
Try the next five days, weeks, months.
I only hope that I'm still growing.

Inertia

Inertia: (noun) a tendency to do nothing or to remain unchanged.

It's the start of the year,
And I already feel myself
Changing, moving, growing
to who I want to be.
Yes, it's frustrating and takes
A lot out of me.
Yes, I have to constantly be more open
to fit life's narrative.
No, I know it's not always going
To be easy.
But I want this year and future
Years to always change and
Move forward.

Not stuck like where I last was.

Another Day

Another day, another second gone.
Another day, another year possibly stuck in this house.
Another day-after-day of work, home and back.
Hopefully there will be another new day
When I can enjoy life again.
Where I can be myself and enjoy going to
Concerts, restaurants, malls, movie theaters, and do some traveling.
Another day to look to the future.

Time

Working, working, working day and night.
Watching time pass by like it's nothing.
Does time exist anymore?
Do I exist still?
I guess time and work are like yin and yang—
Always circling around each other, but never touching.
If the work is worth it, then time doesn't exist.
But if the work is too much or boring, then time becomes a drag.
Make time worth it for you,
Is my advice.
Then you'll feel like growth is slowly moving.

desire

My desire in life,
In this long journey into the world,
Is to have a full experience.
I've always felt out of step,
Like literally stumbling through my life.
I've never felt normal...
I always dodged the incoming bullets
Of stares, and murmurs under people's breaths,
Pretending not to hear their harsh and snide comments.
Now that I've fought this storm of insecurity and public opinion,
I want to live my life the way I deserve it.
With all the happiness my heart can take,
All the love, joy, hope, passion
That I've spent so long trying to grasp.
It's there, I can see it,
Taste it, touch it, feel it.
Because then I won't be dreaming it,
I'll be living it.

Lines from The Twilight Saga: Eclipse (2010), written by Melissa Rosenberg

Part III
Self

Chandelier

Celebrate those moments
Where you are the only one,
The only center,
The only spotlight.
See how every shard of glitter
Is a reason you made it here.
Because what is a chandelier
But broken pieces of glass coming together
To form a new look?
Take a moment to look back on not only yourself,
But also on the shards.
The unruly, sharp edges were necessary.
You can still see the cracks in the mirror,
But it's not ugly; it's a new kind of beautiful.

Self-Check-In

I did a self-check-in today
And found real results.
A body scan
Of emotions, thoughts and feelings
About a particular moment.
To become more in tune with my body.
To not let stress, anxiety or fear carry me over
Until that's all I can see.

I just got back from therapy,
And this session was a lesson.
The release of tension right after
Is a sign of progress.
There's less of a grip of my head, chest and in my face.
My skin has cooled down some,
And my vision has become clearer.
I'm still processing the growth, the evolution,
Of my mindset from the past hour.
For the past four months,
I've been in this state of evolution.
My therapist has been such help
In allowing me to be myself.
I'll be sad and miss her when she leaves in April,
But I know I'll be okay because I'll be able to take what we learned—
What I've learned—
About myself and progress from there.
I've never been able to say that before.
I hope I'll still be able to say that later.

Why Do I Create?

I create for the versions of me that weren't aware
Of themselves, of other people, of people they wanted to be like.
I create for my younger self, who needed a shoulder to lean on.
I create for my teen self, a writer who was so afraid to call herself one.
I create for the person I'm becoming now,
Even if that person isn't a full person yet.
I also create so my thoughts can have something to hold on to,
For them to feel safe and secure so they won't be alone.
I could create for you, but then it wouldn't be free.

Promise

Now that I'm getting some of what I wanted,
It's still overwhelming to accept.
Striving, wishing, hoping, praying,
And falling or failing.
Most of what I've gone through is small
Compared to what others have.
But that's just it, isn't it?
Comparing the life I have
With the life I "should have."
I don't want to keep wondering "what if".
What if it doesn't last?
What if I'm not good enough?
No, I want
To enjoy the fruits of my labor,
Allow them to grow and prosper
Into a beautiful garden,
Where I can enjoy the scenery.
The love and appreciation
Is still something I have to keep to myself.
Like I can't fully bask in my own glory
Unless someone else is there to see it.

I'm still learning to take life in doses,
To accept the ebbs and flows of each day,
To savor every moment
Because not every day is promised.

Healing & Patience

Am I too hard on people
The same way I'm too hard on myself?
I wonder why.
Maybe it stems from insecurity?
Fear of failure?
Fear of being noticed?
Fear of fear itself?

Going to therapy since November,
I've had some revelations about not only myself,
But other people and why they are the way they are.
I still come back to the same habits...
Still have low self-confidence,
Impatience, overprotectiveness, impulsiveness,
But there's also a sense of softness, growth, grace, and embrace.
The constant push and pull of when and how,
Where and when,
Why and where,
Is still something that's on my mind.
As Alessia Cara sings,
Healing and patience are lovers.
And I'm still learning how to combine the two.

Changes

It's been a long week! Filled with
Arguments, feelings of self-doubt, embarrassment, fatigue...

It never stops, does it?
All of it. My frontal lobes are going through
Emotional and personal change,
I can see it. But what does it
look like? I can't say.

This time last year, I was coming out of
A hospital visit,
After I had fainted at work
From taking too many cold pills,
Not resting,
Not eating properly,
And burning myself out for a useless job.
I was waiting for my life to start.

This year, I'm coming out of a better understanding
Of where my heart is.

I'm still waiting for my life to start,
But it's less scary now.

Feeling...

Everything is changing,
Life is changing,
You are changing,
I am forever changing.
The feeling of change
Is a constant episode of pushing outside of a hard shell
Whether it's a cocoon, a room, a house, a building,
A town, city or country.
This shell constantly wants to keep my growth
Locked in, wired shut,
So no one can hear me scream.
When I finally break free,
The sun from outside blares into
My eyes that make me step back for a minute,
Until I adjust.

This constant rebellious force
Makes me want to build more and be more.
It's there for a reason.
Changes become my new feelings,
So I may as well embrace them.

Thank You Notes / Acknowledgments

First, I'd like to thank God always for blessing me with this gift of writing as a vessel for others.

Second, thanks to my family for always believing in me, even when I didn't believe in myself. Thank you Mom, Dad, and my nieces Aniya and Tamani for helping me step out of my comfort zone and try new things. I'd also like to thank my Uncle John for subscribing to my Patreon page!

Thank you also to: My internet friends all over social media for being the best, most loving and dysfunctional fandom family I could ask for: Jen Rodrigues, Jessica Monique, Monica Florence, Amanda, Tash Palo, Brizette, and Packy. Also, I'll thank my online book blogger buddies for their advice and insight: Davona Mapp, Clo (Cuppa Clo), Samantha (Fictionally Sam), and Hannah Sophia Lin (Bookwyrming Thoughts). Who says online friends aren't real friends?!

Next, I'd like to thank my entire team at Reedsy, down to the customer service workers who answered every question I had for my first time publishing a book.

Thank you to my former therapist, Nakato Nteza, for working with me on my mental health journey from November 2020 to April 2021. She was one of the reasons I'm not so afraid to explore different sides of myself, and to be comfortable with being uncomfortable. She had shown me a lot about celebrating the happy moments, making my own decisions, and taking the driver's seat of my life. If you've ever thought about or shied away from therapy, please do it. It'll be hard, but it'll change you forever.

About the Author

Born and raised in New Jersey, Danielle has been writing stories since early childhood. What started from with innocent fairytales in first grade turned into a growing passion that was always one step behind her. After graduating from the University of Phoenix in 2017 with a bachelor's degree in Communications and Journalism, she started her writing journey as a journalist for entertainment media outlets like TV After Dark, Fangirlish and Glitter Magazine. She is a member of the New Jersey Library Association. Currently, she's both writing on her own website, PoetryBooksYA.com, and dodging her father's phone calls about getting a master's degree.